Incredible True
Adventures

REACHING THE
OCEAN FLOOR

BY THERESE SHEA

Gareth Stevens
PUBLISHING

Please visit our website, www.garethstevens.com. For a free color catalog of all our high-quality books, call toll free 1-800-542-2595 or fax 1-877-542-2596.

Library of Congress Cataloging-in-Publication Data

Shea, Therese.
 Reaching the ocean floor / Therese Shea.
     pages cm. — (Incredible true adventures)
 Includes index.
ISBN 978-1-4824-2050-0 (pbk.)
ISBN 978-1-4824-2049-4 (6 pack)
ISBN 978-1-4824-2051-7 (library binding)
1. Deep-sea sounding—Juvenile literature. 2. Ocean bottom—Juvenile literature. 3. Oceanography—Juvenile literature. I. Title.
 GC75.S54 2015
 551.46'8—dc23

                                        2014032733

First Edition

Published in 2015 by
Gareth Stevens Publishing
111 East 14th Street, Suite 349
New York, NY 10003

Copyright © 2015 Gareth Stevens Publishing

Designer: Andrea Davison-Bartolotta
Editor: Kristen Rajczak

Photo credits: Cover, p. 1 littlesam/Shutterstock.com; p. 4 Evgenia Bolyukh/Shutterstock.com;
p. 5 Stocktrek Images/Thinkstock; p. 7 (map) Alfonso de Tomas/Shutterstock.com; p. 7 (background) ded pixto/
Shutterstock.com; p. 8 Time Life Pictures/Mansell/The Life Picture Collection/Getty Images; p. 9 Intrepix/
Shutterstock.com; p. 10 MPI/Getty Images; p. 11 Ann Ronan Pictures/Print Collector/Getty Images;
p. 12 Time Life Pictures/US Navy/The Life Picture Collection/Getty Images; p. 13 SuperStock/Getty Images;
pp. 14, 18 Thomas J. Abercrombie/National Geographic/Getty Images; p. 15 NOAA/Wikimedia Commons;
pp. 16–17 Reinraum/Wikimedia Commons; p. 19 Jack Fletcher/National Geographic/Getty Images;
p. 20 Woods Hole Oceanographic Institution/NASA/Wikimedia Commons; p. 21 Mr. John F. Williams/
courtesy of the US Navy; p. 22 Keipher McKennie/WireImage/Getty Images; p. 23 Zuckerberg/
Wikimedia Commons; p. 25 Jason LaVeris/FilmMagic/Getty Images; p. 27 (both) John M. Heller/Getty Images;
p. 28 Efired/Shutterstock.com; p. 29 Mass Communication Specialist Seaman Chelsea Kennedy/
courtesy of the US Navy.

Printed in the United States of America

CPSIA compliance information: Batch #CW15GS: For further information contact Gareth Stevens, New York, New York at 1-800-542-2595.

Contents »»»»»»»»»»»

Words in the glossary appear in **bold** type the first time they are used in the text.

THE LAST FRONTIER

Humanity has succeeded in reaching the most challenging places. People have climbed Mount Everest, reached the North and South Poles, and even walked on the moon. Armed with **technology**, explorers of today seem almost unstoppable in their quests to make the unknown known. However, there's one **environment** that has proven to be very hard to explore—Earth's oceans.

Incredibly, it's thought that we've only explored 5 or 6 percent of the ocean floor and just one half of 1 percent of the entire ocean! Why have we seen so little of this part of Earth? As you'll read, the journey into the ocean, especially the ocean floor, is full of dangers.

Water, Water Everywhere

One reason we've explored so little of the ocean is because it's so large. The oceans and their seas cover about 70 percent of the planet's surface. The oceans and sea ice make up about 97.957 percent of all the water on Earth. Since liquid water is needed for life, it's lucky we have the oceans!

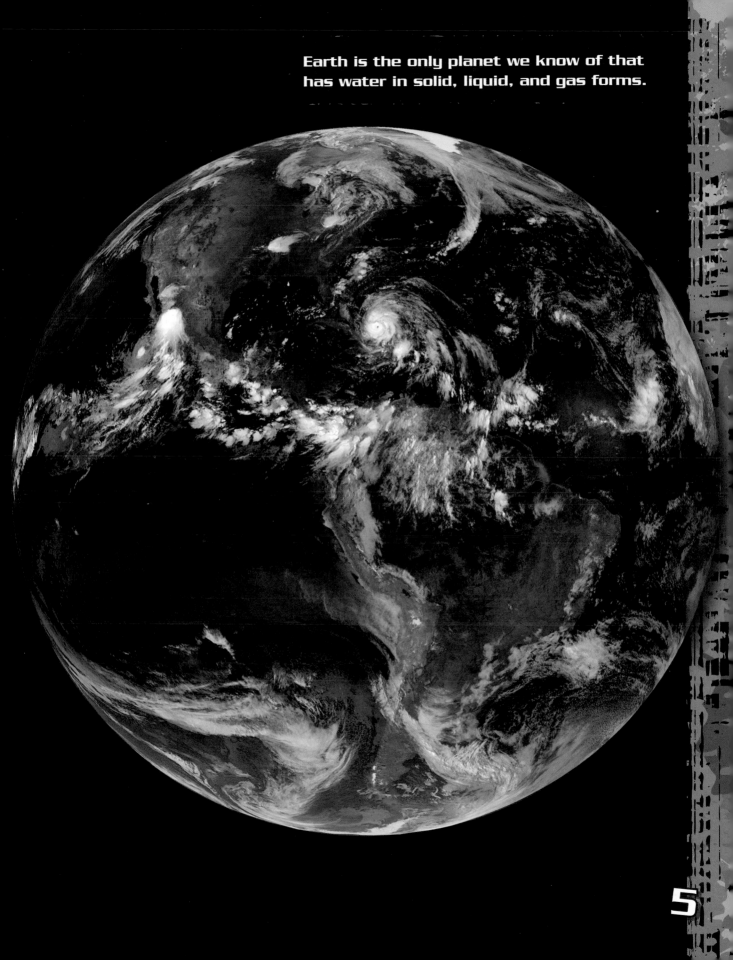

Earth is the only planet we know of that has water in solid, liquid, and gas forms.

WATER WORLD

Around the continents are shallow areas called continental shelves. Continental shelves covered in **sediment** extend out to steeper continental slopes, which lead down to an area called the continental rise. Finally, the continental rise **descends** to the ocean floor, the abyssal plain. However, it's not all flat there. Like the rest of Earth's surface, it has tall mountains, wide plains, narrow valleys, and other landforms.

The average depth of the world's oceans is about 12,459 feet (3,795 m), or as tall as some Rocky Mountain peaks. Explorers need special underwater craft to handle the dangers that can occur at those depths.

Just One Ocean?

Earth contains one ocean. However, since it's so large, people find it easier to divide it into several bodies of water. The boundaries between them aren't always easy to identify. Some people name only four oceans: the Atlantic, Pacific, Indian, and Arctic. Others call the southern waters of the Pacific, the Atlantic, and the Indian Oceans the Southern Ocean.

Bathymetry is the science of underwater topography, which is the study and mapping of land features. This is mostly done through taking measurements of the features of the ocean floor.

Deep Waters

ocean	average depth
Atlantic	12,890 feet (3,929 m)
Pacific	14,040 feet (4,279 m)
Indian	12,990 feet (3,959 m)
Arctic	3,950 feet (1,204 m)

Arctic Ocean

Atlantic Ocean

Pacific Ocean

Indian Ocean

CHALLENGER DEEP

In 1875, the HMS *Challenger* was undergoing a global voyage to study the oceans. The ship carried about 144 miles (232 km) of rope! The crew used weights attached to the rope to measure ocean depth in different places. Using this method, they found an area in the western Pacific Ocean thought to be the world's deepest point, now called Challenger Deep. The crew measured Challenger Deep at 26,850 feet (8,184 m).

In 1951, another ship called HMS *Challenger* used sonar to measure the same place. This time, the measurement was 35,761 feet (10,900 m). Modern sonar measures this point's depth at 36,070 feet (10,994 km).

HMS *Challenger* (1875)

Sonar

Sonar is one of the reasons we know about the landscape of the ocean floor even though we haven't explored it much. "Sonar" stands for **so**und **n**avigation **a**nd **r**anging. While using sonar, scientists send sound waves toward the ocean floor. The waves echo back at different times, depending on the depth of the object they hit.

Challenger Deep is located in the Mariana (or Marianas) Trench. A trench is a long, narrow valley on the ocean floor.

Asia

Pacific Ocean

Mariana Trench

Challenger Deep ●

Australia

SUBMERSIBLES

To explore great ocean depths further, people created special underwater vessels. Submersibles are watercraft **designed** to travel to greater depths than submarines. The deeper you go under the surface, the greater the pressure of the water pushing on you. Submersibles are built to withstand the great pressure the ocean applies to objects in deep waters.

The first submersibles for exploration were attached to a ship by cable or rope. Crew on the ship raised and lowered the submersible. However, this wasn't possible at the greatest depths. Swiss scientist Auguste Piccard thought of a way a submersible could operate by itself. He called the new kind of vessel a bathyscaphe.

1860s submersible

Early Submarines

The first submarine, made of wood covered by leather, was built in the 1620s by Dutch inventor Cornelis Drebbel. Powered by oars, it traveled about 15 feet (4.6 m) below the surface of the water. Many others tried to perfect a submarine design in the 1700s and later. Submarines were even used in the American Revolution!

11

THE TRIESTE

Piccard and his son Jacques designed an improved bathyscaphe and launched it in 1953. Called the *Trieste* (TREE-ehs-tah), the US Navy heard about it and bought it in 1958. With the help of the Piccards, they prepared it for the first descent into the deepest waters in the world—the Challenger Deep.

The *Trieste* had two main parts: a container about 50 feet (15.2 m) long filled with gasoline and a round cabin underneath about 6.5 feet (2 m) wide for two passengers. Air tanks kept the vessel afloat. When the tanks were filled with water, the *Trieste* would sink under the weight of 9 tons (8 mt) of iron pieces it carried!

Jacques Piccard

The Underwater Balloon

Why was the Trieste loaded with 22,500 gallons (83,270 l) of gasoline? Gasoline is lighter, or less dense, than water. Auguste Piccard figured out that when the iron was released from the vessel, the gasoline would carry the Trieste to the surface. The bathyscaphe was described as an "underwater hot air balloon."

The round cabin on the underside of the *Trieste* had a small window through which to observe the ocean. The window was made of Plexiglas, which is a thick, solid type of plastic.

It was essential the bathyscaphe could hold up to the pressure of deep ocean waters. According to one source, the pressure in Challenger Deep is about the same a person would feel if 50 jets were placed on top of them! The passenger cabin's steel walls were 5 inches (12.7 cm) thick to protect the pilots.

After months of improvements to the vessel, the *Trieste* was ready for its journey on January 23, 1960. In the cabin were Jacques Piccard and Don Walsh, a 28-year-old submarine officer in the US Navy. When the two men were ready to descend, they filled the craft's air tanks with water.

Rocky Start

The ocean waters that day in 1960 were very rough, and the journey was almost called off. However, the US Navy and the *Trieste*'s crew decided to continue. The navy had searched for the right spot to place the vessel by throwing explosives in the water and timing the echo back!

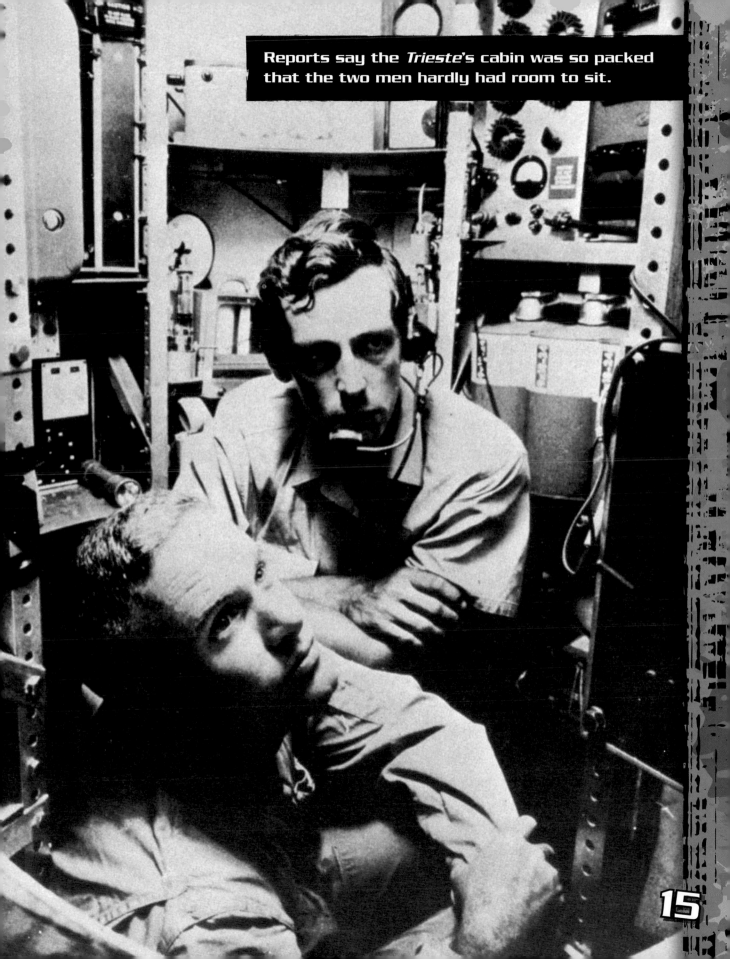

Reports say the *Trieste*'s cabin was so packed that the two men hardly had room to sit.

The journey downward was slow. The *Trieste* traveled about 3 feet (0.9 m) per second. At about 27,000 feet (8,230 m) down, the viewing window cracked and shook the whole vessel! Luckily, there were no leaks. Piccard and Walsh decided to keep going but began to descend even slower into the dark, cold waters. The temperature in the *Trieste*'s cabin fell to 45°F (7°C).

After 4 hours and 48 minutes, the *Trieste* finally touched down on the ocean floor of Challenger Deep. Piccard and Walsh were at the lowest place on Earth, a place no one else had ever reached. The two men shook hands.

interior controls of the *Trieste*

Sights and Sounds

Walsh and Piccard could hear many sounds: Pressure acted on the outside of the craft, making it groan. Inside the *Trieste*, the gasoline cooled and became denser. Through the viewing window, the pilots could see glowing sea creatures that they said looked like "snow." Unfortunately, when the ship hit bottom, it created sediment clouds that blocked their view.

The men aboard the *Trieste* used a sonar-based system to talk to people on the surface. It took 7 seconds for a message to travel up!

sonar

Piccard and Walsh thought they saw a flatfish out the window. Piccard later wrote: "Here, in an instant, was the answer that biologists had asked for the decades. Could life exist in the greatest depths of the ocean? It could!" Scientists had thought the pressure at such depths would crush the bones of fish. Today, people are still unsure if the pilots really saw a flatfish or a different kind of creature such as an eel.

After 20 minutes, the *Trieste*'s crew started the journey back. They rid the vessel of some iron pieces and began to rise slowly. The ascent took another 3 hours and 15 minutes.

What Happened to the Trieste?

When they reached the surface again, Walsh and Piccard opened the cabin's door and felt the sun's warmth on their faces. They had successfully completed their task. The *Trieste* was used again several times to locate sunken submarines and collect underwater photos. People can see the bathyscaphe today at the Navy Museum in Washington, DC.

President Dwight D. Eisenhower presents Walsh and Piccard with an award for their brave journey in this photo.

19

ROBOT EXPLORERS

In the years since the *Trieste* completed its amazing journey, scientists have invented robots to make similar trips. The Deep Submergence Lab at the Woods Hole Oceanographic Institution (WHOI) built *Nereus*, a robotic submersible, in 2008. It descended into Challenger Deep on its first mission, bringing back ocean creatures for study.

However, in 2014, the *Nereus* proved the dangers of the deep while exploring Kermadec Trench off New Zealand. The vessel was about 6.2 miles (10 km) into the trench when scientists lost contact with it. Pieces of the *Nereus* soon appeared on the water's surface. It's believed the *Nereus* was destroyed by the great pressure under the water.

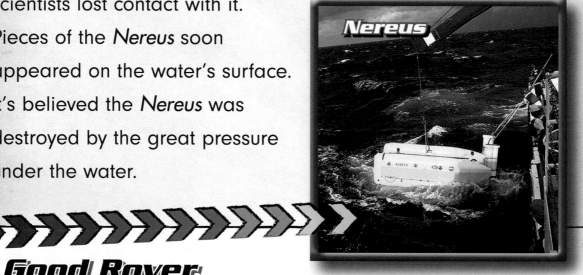

Nereus

Good Rover

The Benthic Rover is a car-sized robot that crawls along the ocean floor. It allowed scientists at the Monterey Bay Aquarium **Research** Institute to study oxygen levels over 3 years at about 13,000 feet (4,000 m) below the surface. The scientists are trying to figure out through these levels how **climate change** affects the ocean food supply.

WHOI uses Remote
Environmental Monitoring
Units (REMUS) to map and
observe the deep waters
of the ocean.

DEEPSEA CHALLENGER

Filmmaker James Cameron became the first person to reach the depths of Challenger Deep solo. His vessel, a submersible called the *Deepsea Challenger*, dove 35,787 feet (10,908 m) to establish a new world record for a trip taken by one person on March 26, 2012.

Cameron said he sometimes felt fear thinking of the journey ahead. However, on the day of the descent, he felt only "childlike excitement."

It took Cameron and a crew of scientists about 8 years to create his vessel and prepare for the journey. The result was that the *Deepsea Challenger* was much faster and lighter than the *Trieste*. It was also fitted with cameras to capture the ocean environment and video screens that helped Cameron see his surroundings.

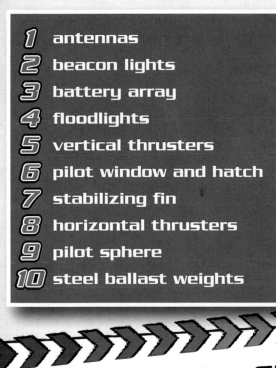

1. antennas
2. beacon lights
3. battery array
4. floodlights
5. vertical thrusters
6. pilot window and hatch
7. stabilizing fin
8. horizontal thrusters
9. pilot sphere
10. steel ballast weights

"A Walnut in Its Shell"

In a June 2013 *National Geographic* article, James Cameron described his vessel's cabin: "The pilot's chamber is a 43-inch-**diameter** steel ball, and I'm packed into it like a walnut in its shell, my knees pushed up in a hunched sitting position, my head pressed down by the curve of the hull... To me it just feels snug and comforting."

Two and half hours after Cameron began his descent into Challenger Deep, he touched down on the ocean floor. He said it looked like another world, though one without much life. He didn't see fish or any creature longer than an inch (2.5 cm), though he observed some shrimplike animals.

The pressure of the ocean depths caused problems for his submersible, though. He wasn't able to use the robotic arm to capture samples. However, he collected sediment in

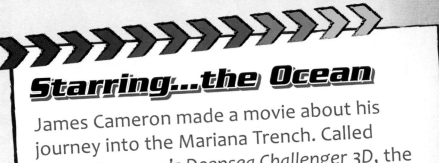

Starring...the Ocean

James Cameron made a movie about his journey into the Mariana Trench. Called *James Cameron's Deepsea Challenger 3D*, the movie contains footage that he captured while 7 miles (11 km) beneath the surface as well as the story of the preparation and hard work it took to get to that point.

which scientists have found tiny forms of life. Cameron sees his journey as the first of many, saying that there "is a vast frontier down there that's going to take us a while to understand."

Compare the Crafts

Trieste (1960)	Deepsea Challenger (2012)
weighs 150 tons (136 mt)	weighs 11.8 tons (10.7 mt)
two pilots	single pilot
descent: 4 hours, 48 minutes	descent: 2 hours, 30 minutes
ascent: 3 hours, 15 minutes	ascent: 1 hour, 10 minutes
unable to take photos	8 cameras, an "arm" to the outside, sample box
20 minutes at the bottom	3 hours at the bottom

Cameron was supposed to be able to spend 6 hours in the trench. However, a fluid leak in the submersible made him leave earlier. It coated the viewing window, making it hard to see.

Next to Descend?

James Cameron and his team had some competition as they prepared for Challenger Deep. At least three other teams were planning to do the same and may yet do so. They include explorer Chris Welsh, who plans to "fly" the *DeepFlight Challenger*, which has wings and a tail like a plane, into Challenger Deep in just 140 minutes.

The DOER Marine company is planning a scientific research vessel with a robotic arm that can be used in many ocean environments. The submersible will hold 72 hours of oxygen.

Triton Submarines is building crafts that can reach great ocean depths, too. They plan to sell tickets to passengers: $250,000 a seat!

Watching the Waters

The X-Prize Foundation has announced a $2 million prize for the invention of a **sensor** to monitor, or watch over, all depths of ocean waters. While coastal environments suffer from pollution, not much is known about deeper places like Challenger Deep. A future explorer may place a sensor in the Mariana Trench to send readings to the surface.

Chris Welsh and businessman Richard Branson (shown above) plan on exploring the deepest parts of each of the world's oceans.

KEEP DIVING

Why is further ocean exploration and discovery so important? As many as 2.6 billion people depend on the ocean for food, so knowledge of the ocean's health is essential. Additionally, the ocean can impact us in other ways: One of the species brought back by James Cameron seems promising to help fight **Alzheimer's disease**. Could other medical treatments and even cures be found on the ocean floor?

As technology progresses in robotic and manned submersibles, we'll find out the answer to this question and more. Our unexplored ocean floor undoubtedly holds more surprises than we can guess.

So Many More

It's thought that between 700,000 and 1 million species live in the ocean. And between one-third and two-thirds of those have yet to be found and recorded! These aren't just tiny forms of life. Scientists think there may be as many as eight unknown species of dolphins and whales.

In the future, ocean explorers may walk the ocean floor in suits like this.

Glossary ⟫⟫⟫⟫⟫⟫⟫⟫⟫⟫

Alzheimer's disease: a brain disease that causes memory loss, problems with thinking, and other harmful changes

climate change: long-term change in Earth's climate, caused partly by human activities such as burning oil and natural gas

descend: to go downward

design: the pattern or shape of something. Also, to create the pattern or shape of something.

diameter: the distance from one side of a round object to another through its center

environment: the natural world in which a plant or animal lives

research: studying to find something new

sediment: matter, such as stones and sand, that is carried onto land or into the water by wind, water, or land movement

sensor: a tool that can detect changes in its surroundings

technology: the way people do something using tools and the tools that they use

For More Information ▶▶▶▶▶▶▶▶▶▶▶▶▶

Books

Aleshire, Peter. *Ocean Ridges and Trenches.* New York, NY: Chelsea House, 2007.

Claybourne, Anna. *Deep Oceans.* Chicago, IL: Heinemann Library, 2008.

Yount, Lisa. *Modern Marine Science: Exploring the Deep.* New York, NY: Chelsea House, 2006.

Websites

Deepsea Challenge
deepseachallenge.com
Find out more information about James Cameron's expedition.

Submersibles
oceanexplorer.noaa.gov/technology/subs/subs.html
Read about several different submersibles.

Underwater Research Vehicles
www.divediscover.whoi.edu/robotics/deep.html
Examine a fascinating diagram about water pressure and ocean exploration.

Index